1 MONTH OF
FREE
READING

at
www.ForgottenBooks.com

By purchasing this book you are eligible for one month membership to ForgottenBooks.com, giving you unlimited access to our entire collection of over 1,000,000 titles via our web site and mobile apps.

To claim your free month visit:

www.forgottenbooks.com/free1112405

ISBN 978-0-331-36606-8
PIBN 11112405

Annual Reports

of the Town Officers

of

HANCOCK, N. H.

For the year ending
January 31

1929

TRANSCRIPT PRINTING COMPANY . PETERBOROUGH, N. H.

Town Officers

Moderator, George W. Goodhue.

Town Clerk, Charles A. Brown.

Town Treasurer, Ernest L. Adams.

Selectmen, George H. Fogg, Maurice S. Tuttle, Charles E. Adams.

Collector of Taxes, Chester F. Dutton.

Road Agent, Thomas F. Hugron.

Overseer of Poor, Wendell D. Crowell.

Health Officer, Wendell D. Crowell.

Common Commissioners, William D. Fogg, Charles A. Sheldon, William J. Hayden.

Water Commissioners, Harry M. Sheldon, William E. Putnam, William D. Fogg.

Library Trustees, Annie L. Putnam, Margaret Perry, Frank Pearson.

Supervisors of Check List, Charles A. Sheldon, John E. Hadley, Fred C. Eaton.

Trustees of Trust Funds, William D. Fogg, Edson K. Upton, Ernest L. Adams.

Electric Light Committee, Ernest L. Adams, William E. Putnam, Edson K. Upton.

Auditors, Karl G. Upton, George W. Goodhue.

Surveyors of Wood and Lumber, Harry M. Sheldon, Joseph Quinn.

Police, Ernest L. Adams, Chief; Wendell D. Crowell.

Agent for Town Clock, John E. Hadley.

Cemetery Committee, John E. Hadley, Charles P. Hayward, William J. Hayden.

Sexton, John E. Hadley.

Library Building Committee, Charles E. Adams, Margaret Perry, William E. Putnam.

Memorial Day Committee, George W. Weston, Chairman.

SCHOOL DISTRICT OFFICERS

Moderator, George W. Goodhue.

Clerk, Alice M. Brown.

School Board, Cora F. Otis, William D. Fogg, Ella C. Ware.

Auditors, Karl G. Upton, George W. Goodhue.

Treasurer, Ernest L. Adams.

SELECTMEN'S REPORT

Valuation of town by invoice taken
    April 1, 1928:

Land and buildings	$712,795	00
146 horses	11,685	00
5 mules	375	00
240 cows	16,180	00
52 neat stock	2,275	00
158 sheep	1,578	00
35 hogs	500	00
4623 fowls	5,657	00
3 portable mills	2,500	00
25 boats and launches	1,300	00
Wood and lumber	30,170	00
Gasoline pumps and tanks	3,100	00
Stock in trade	13,675	00
Mills and machinery	6,700	00

    Total valuation $808,490 00

Property tax	$20,212	25
332 poll taxes	664	00
National Bank stock tax	108	60

    Total tax $20,984 85
Rate per cent. on valuation, $2.50.

MONEY RAISED BY TAX

State tax	$1,997	10
County tax	1,551	75
Highways and bridges	2,500	00
Town poor	1,000	00
Trunk Line construction	1,000	00
Trunk Line maintenance	750	00
Town patrol	400	00
State Aid maintenance	100	00
Lighting streets	710	00
Town notes	700	00
Memorial Day	150	00
Schools	8,950	00

Overlay	403	40
Polls, 332	664	00
National Bank tax	108	60

Total		$20,984 85

APPROPRIATIONS

Trunk Line construction	$1,000	00
Trunk Line maintenance	500	00
Highway and bridges	500	00
Middle Road repairs	500	00
Reservoir repairs	300	00
Monument plate	125	00
Old Home Week	100	00
Dental clinic	50	00
Publicity pictures	12	75
		$3,087 75

ASSETS OF THE TOWN

Cash on hand	$3,900	09
140 copies of Town Histories	339	00
Due from tax collector, 1928	355	01
Due from State, state aid maintenance	2	84
Due from State, Trunk Line maintenance	7	51
Due from State, Trunk Line construction	5	47
Bounties	33	80
		$4,643 72

LIABILITIES OF THE TOWN

Due to School District, dog licenses	$182	47
Unexpended Trunk Line maintenance	2	50
Unexpended State aid	2	84

Unexpended Trunk Line construction	1 82	
Water notes	4,500 00	
Electric Line notes	9,100 00	
		$13,789 63

ACCOUNT WITH STATE

State tax	$1,997 10

CREDITS

Insurance tax	$ 75	
Railroad tax	209 79	
Savings Bank tax	1,370 72	
Check to balance State tax	415 84	
		$1,997 10

Payments

TOWN OFFICERS' SALARIES

Ephraim Weston, as selectman	$40 00	
George H. Fogg, as selectman	203 00	
Maurice S. Tuttle, as selectman	276 89	
Charles E. Adams, as selectman	155 00	
Charles A. Brown, town clerk	119 55	
Chester F. Dutton, tax collector	170 00	
Ernest L. Adams, town treasurer	75 00	
Wendell D. Crowell, Overseer of Poor and Board of Health	50 00	
John E. Hadley, care of clock	40 00	
George W. Goodhue, auditor 2 years	15 00	
Karl G. Upton, auditor 2 years	15 00	
		$1,159 44

TOWN OFFICERS' EXPENSES

350 Town reports	$132 85	
Shirley R. Cross, appraising Electric Line	69 46	
New England Tel. & Tel. Co., phone	10 00	
Town officers' supplies	130 34	
N. H. Tax Assessors' Asso., dues	2 00	
Transcript Printing Co., invoices	64 65	
Ephraim Weston, expenses	12 20	
George H. Fogg, expenses and auto	43 06	
Maurice S. Tuttle, expenses and auto	17 70	
Charles E. Adams, expenses and auto	12 00	
Ernest L. Adams, expenses	4 65	
James F. Phelps Co., officers' bonds	40 00	
Legal advice	12 00	
Karl G. Upton, clerical work	8 00	
		$558 91

ELECTION AND REGISTRATION

Charles A. Sheldon, supervisors	$58 00	
John E. Hadley, supervisor, 1927	4 00	
George W. Goodhue, moderator	10 00	
Charles P. Hayward, ballot clerk	12 00	
Thomas B. Manning, ballot clerk	12 00	
Wendell D. Crowell, ballot clerk	12 00	
William D. Fogg, ballot clerk	12 00	
		$120 00

TOWN HALL

Public Service Co. of N. H., lights	$42 37	
Supplies	1 81	
Repairs	81 37	
Wood	17 06	
Painting Town Hall and clock	545 00	
		$687 61

POLICE DEPARTMENT

Ernest L. Adams, police	$29 00	
Ernest L. Adams, care of tramps	12 50	
Wendell D. Crowell, police	6 00	
		$47 50

FIRE DEPARTMENT

Ernest L. Adams, fire warden	$23 40

BOUNTIES

Ephraim Weston	$5 20	
George H. Fogg	9 00	
Maurice S. Tuttle	11 40	
Charles E. Adams	8 20	
		$33 80

DAMAGE BY DOGS

Harry M. Sheldon, 2 sheep	$20 00

HEALTH DEPARTMENT

Paid to Health Officer	$17 98

VITAL STATISTICS

Paid G. D. Tibbetts	$1 00

STATE AID MAINTENANCE

W. A. Osgood	$178 99	
Gifford Merchant	82 48	
		$261 47

Trunk Line Maintenance

L. J. Parker	$19 80	
Fred H. Prince	92 23	
Gifford Merchant	1,727 85	
W. A. Osgood	720 40	
		$2,560 28

Town Maintenance

R. B. Harrington	$83 33	
Thomas F. Hugron	4,367 69	
American Tar Co.	96 80	
		$4,547 82

Town Patrol

Gifford Merchant	$100 75	
W. A. Osgood	689 99	
		$790 74

Winter Roads

R. B. Harrington	$40 08	
F. E. Everett, balance due State, snow fence	17 09	
T. F. Hugron	197 49	
		$254 66

Street Lights

Public Service Co. of N. H.	$701 40

GENERAL EXPENSE, HIGHWAY DEPARTMENT

H. F. Nichols, repairs on tractor	$50 00	
W. M. Hanson, repairs on tractor	25 00	
Supplies	4 50	
Tool house	54 52	
Bridge signs	36 20	
T. F. Hugron, insurance	77 33	
A. Hill, watering tub 1928	3 00	
G. H. Haskell, watering tub, 1927 and 1928	6 00	
		$256 55

LIBRARY

G. H. Cole, repairs	$27 35

TOWN POOR

W. D. Crowell, overseer	$534 71

HUBBARD LEGACY

Deserving poor	$110 00

COUNTY POOR

Wm. G. Fisher, auto to Grasmere	$10 00

MEMORIAL DAY

George W. Weston, chairman	$150 00

OLD HOME DAY

Bessie Hanson, treasurer	$100 00

SOLDIERS' MONUMENT

Lowell Monument Co. $125 00

SPECIAL APPROPRIATIONS

Karl G. Upton, framing pictures $12 75

CEMETERIES

Carrie A. Wilds, housing hearse	$ 8 00	
W. J. Hayden	164 00	
C. P. Hayward	57 60	
		$229 60

ELECTRIC LINE

E. K. Upton, new extensions and
   repairs $8,305 05

REFUND

C. A. Brown, overpayment on auto
   permits 1927 $25 44

INTEREST

First Nat'l Bank, Peterboro, N.H.	$191 67	
Trustees of Trust Funds, Electric line and water notes	438 25	
Peterboro Savings Bank	85 00	
		$714 92

TRUNK LINE CONSTRUCTION

Gifford Merchant $11,550 10

TEMPORARY LOANS

First Nat'l Bank, Peterboro, N.H.
  in anticipation of taxes $10,000 00
Electric line   2,000 00
Peterboro Savings Bank, electric
  line   1,000 00
                                 ——————— $13,000 00

TOWN NOTES

Trustees of trust funds $1,950 00

SINKING FUND

Trustees of trust funds, for electric
  line $800 00

STATE AND COUNTY

County tax $1,551 75
State Treasurer, balance due on
  State tax   415 84
                                 ——————— $1,967 59

SCHOOLS

Hancock School District appropria-
  tions $8,950 00
Dog licenses   83 73
                                 ——————— $9,033 73

WATER DEPARTMENT

W. D. Fogg, labor and supplies	$7 25	
W. E. Putnam, services	15 50	
W. E. Putnam, cleaning reservoir	23 00	
Transcript Printing Co., waterbills	3 75	
		$49 50

RECAPITULATION

Town officers' salaries	$1,159 44
Town officers' expenses	558 91
Election and registration	120 00
Town Hall	687 61
Police Department	47 50
Fire Department	23 40
Bounties	33 80
Damage by dogs	20 00
Health Department	17 98
Vital statistics	1 00
State Aid maintenance	261 47
Trunk Line maintenance	2,560 28
Town maintenance	4,547 82
Town patrol	790 74
Winter roads	254 66
Street lighting	701 40
General expense of Highway Department, including watering tubs	256 55
Library	27 35
Town poor	534 71
Hubbard Legacy	110 00
County poor	10 00
Memorial Day	150 00
Old Home Day	100 00
Soldiers' Monument	125 00
Special appropriations	12 75
Cemeteries	229 60
Electric line, new extensions and repairs	8,305 05
Refund	25 44
Interest	714 92
Trunk Line construction	11,550 10

Temporary loans	13,000 00	
Term notes	1,950 00	
Sinking fund for electric line	800 00	
State and county	1,967 59	
Schools	9,033 73	
Water Department	49 50	
		$60,738 30

Respectfully submitted,
GEORGE H. FOGG
MAURICE S. TUTTLE
CHARLES E. ADAMS
Selectmen of Hancock

TOWN CLERK'S REPORT

Year Ending January 31, 1929

DR.

No. male dogs licensed, 58 at $2.00	$114 67	
No. female dogs licensed, 16 at $5.00	80 00	
No. Sp. female dogs licensed, 6 at $2.00	12 00	
No. Kennel licenses, 1 at $12.00	12 00	
		$218 67

CR.

Town clerk's fee, 81 licenses at 20¢	$16 20	
Paid treasurer	202 47	
		$218 67

DR.

1928 auto permits issued Feb. 1 to Dec. 31, 1928 126		
1929 auto permits issued Jan. 1 to Jan. 31, 1929 115		
Amount collected	$976 20	$976 20

CR.

Paid treasurer	$976 20	$976 20

Respectfully submitted,
CHARLES A. BROWN
Town Clerk

TREASURER'S REPORT

E. L. ADAMS, TREASURER, IN ACCOUNT WITH THE TOWN OF
HANCOCK, FEB. 1, 1929

Received:

Balance from 1928	$3,755	41
W. J. Hayden, revenue from town scales	25	95
D. O. Devens, revenue from town scales	44	10
Annie ·L. Putnam, town histories sold	14	50
C. A. Brown, auto permits	976	20
C. A. Brown, dog licenses	202	47
Margaret Perry, use of tractor	42	00
Wendell D. Crowell, refund from county	21	00
Public Service Co. of New Hampshire, revenue from Electric line	2,087	48
Almon Hill, Holden's goods sold	8	00
Wendell D. Crowell, refund on telephone	2	75
Annie L. Putnam, cemetery book		30
Sargent Camp, repairs on Electric Line	11	65
C. A. Brown (judge), court fines	15	00
George W. Weston, refund on Memorial Day	28	97
State Treasurer, forest fire bill	10	75
First National Bank of Peterborough, temporary loans	12,000	00
Peterborough Savings Bank notes	5,000	00
J. A. Page, use of Town Hall	5	00
Thomas Coughlan, use of Town Hall	22	50
C. A. Brown, refund on Eastman's bill	2	95
G. Merchant, reinforcement irons	10	08
G. Merchant, money lent	100	00
G. Merchant, repairs on tractor	25	00
Trustees of Trust Funds for Town Poor	95	00
New England Tel. & Tel. Co., half interest in Electric Line poles	3,225	00

Hillsboro County, refund on Fisher's bill	10	00
State Treasurer, trunk line construction and maintenance	10,592	23
State Treasurer, town road maintenance	808	93
State Treasurer, tax on interest and dividends	3,568	34
State Treasurer, bounties	44	60
John E. Hadley, taxes 1921	1	12
Chester F. Dutton, taxes 1927	369	04
Interest on taxes 1927	2	21
Chester F. Dutton, taxes 1928	20,601	47
Chester F. Dutton, water rentals	908	39

Total receipts	$64,638 39
Paid: Selectmen's orders	60,738 30
Balance on hand	$3,900 09

ERNEST L. ADAMS, Treasurer

Treasurer's Report of Town Common Account

Balance on hand	$7 20	
Received from Trustees of Trust Funds	150 00	
		$157 20
Paid:		
Hancock Garage for sharpening lawn mowers	$4 00	
W. J. Hayden, work on Common	112 00	
Almon Hill, labor and steel for seats on Common	28 43	
Frank A. Wood & Sons, lumber for seats on Common	2 73	
W. D. Fogg, labor on seats on Common	4 50	
H. M. Sheldon, lumber for seats on Common	3 84	
		$155 50
Balance on hand		$1 70

ERNEST L. ADAMS
Treasurer

Report of Tax Collector for the Year Ending Feb. 1, 1929

Amount of Warrant	$20,984 85	
Added to Warrant	12 00	
Total to collect		$20,996 85
Abatements:		
Standard Oil	$21 87	
Harry Newell	2 00	
Nellie Newell	2 00	
Cornelia Twiss	2 00	
Abbie Barrus	2 50	
Tony Igo	2 00	
George Fish	2 00	
Laura Fish	2 00	
Hiram Marshall	2 00	
Amy Marshall	2 00	
Actual Warrant		$20,956 48
Paid E. L. Adams		$20,601 47
Balance due town Feb. 1, 1929		$355 01

CHESTER F. DUTTON
Collector

WATER RENT STATEMENT

Warrant, July 1, 1928 to July 1, 1929	$910 06
Balance due from last year	183 63
	$1,093 69
Paid E. L. Adams	908 39
Due town Feb. 1, 1929	$185 30

Water Commissioners' Report

Fiscal year rentals July 1, 1928 to July 1, 1929, in the amount of $910.06 have been committed to Chester F. Dutton for collection.

As an illustration of how this service has increased by new

and additional equipment, it may be of interest at this time
to refer to report for year 1919, when rentals amounted to
$659.26 and we are now presenting a report showing an in-
crease of 38 per cent.

Owing to the favorable weather last fall we were able to
have the brush and leaves around the reservoir and road to
the highway cleaned up. Total cost for same was $28.50.

Respectfully submitted,
H. M. SHELDON
WILLIAM E. PUTNAM
W. D. FOGG

Report of Electric Lighting Committee

The lighting system has been extended to the Haskell place
in the west part of the town, to the Johnson place on the
Peterborough road, to the Hubbard place near Cavender
Station, and to the Gullefer place in the north east part of
the town, approximately five and one-half miles of new line,
at a cost of $4,649.79 to the town. To date, these extensions
have added nine new customers. The three phase line has
also been extended from the village to Johnson's mill.

The town has received $2,087.48 from the Public Service
Company of New Hampshire which is the gross income for
the year for the line.

We have not as yet received an offer for the town's interest in the lighting system equal to the price set by the voters
at the last annual town meeting but negotiations are still
pending.

We expect to be able to close a contract with the Public
Service Company of New Hampshire for a continuation of
their service at a more favorable rate.

We herewith submit a detailed account of the cost of extensions, repairs and general expenses.

NEW EXTENSIONS AND SERVICES

Amount appropriated	$4,820 34	
Received from New Eng. Tel & Tel.	3,225 00	
		$8,045 34

Paid:

A. T. Appleton, labor	$3,842 90	
Wetmore-Savage Co., supplies	1,906 94	
H. C. Bolton, poles	1,866 90	
Public Service Co. of N. H., labor	138 50	
D. O. Devens, supplies	13 16	
W. M. Hanson, trucking	8 70	
Chas. D. Wilds, labor	5 08	
James T. Phelps Co., insurance	26 60	
Geo. Barthlein, labor	1 50	
C. S. Ellinwood, labor	9 00	
E. C. Hugron, labor	11 50	
Osgood Estate, storage	20 00	
E. K. Upton, freight and express	62 51	
E. K. Upton, telephone and postage	17 05	
E. K. Upton, use of auto	35 00	
E. K. Upton, services on committee	70 00	
W. E. Putnam, services on committee	10 00	
		$8,045 34

Net Cost of New Extensions and Services

Total bills paid		$8,045 34
Material on hand Jan. 31, 1928	$44 85	
Material on hand Jan. 31, 1929	215 50	
Gain in material on hand		$170 65
		$7,874 79
Less amount received from New Eng. Tel. & Tel.		3,225 00
Net cost of new extensions and services		$4,649 79

Repairs and General Expenses

Received from selectmen		$259 71

Paid:

Public Service Co. of N. H., labor	$153 94	
E. K. Upton, services on committee	30 00	
E. K. Upton, paid telephones	8 50	
E. L. Adams, services on committee	10 00	

W. E. Putnam, services on commit-
    tee   30 00

W. E. Putnam, telephone and R. R.
    expense   27 27

                                                   $259 71

Less amount received from Sargent
    Camp, Inc.   11 65

Net cost to town $248 06

Respectfully submitted,
        ERNEST L. ADAMS
        WILLIAM E. PUTNAM
        EDSON K. UPTON

Overseer of the Poor

Received from treasurer $534 71

Paid:

Hillsborough County Farm	$478 54	
J. Coughlin, labor	14 31	
J. Quinn, transportation	10 00	
A. Hill, rent and wood	17 50	
C. A. Upton, groceries	14 36	
		$534 71

        WENDELL D. CROWELL
          Overseer of the Poor

Board of Health

Received from treasurer $17 98

Paid C. A. Upton, groceries $17 98

        WENDELL D. CROWELL
             Health Officer

Report of Memorial Day Committee, 1928

EXPENSES

Paid:
Band	$50 00	
Supper for Band	20 00	
Dinner for Wilton Post	20 00	
Rings (100)	5 13	
Telephone	85	
Flags (2 doz.)	2 00	
String	30	
Programs	2 75	
Wilton Post	10 00	
Peterborough Post	10 00	
Total		$121 03
Balance from $150		$28 97

GEORGE W. WESTON

Chairman

Treasurer's Report of Old Home Day Committee, 1928

Receipts:
Balance from 1927	$91 31	
Town appropriation	100 00	
Proceeds from dance	169 05	
Proceeds from sale of ice cream	24 04	
Donation from Mrs. Hayward of Wilton, N. H.	2 00	
Donation from Mr. Davis of Bristol, N. H.	3 00	
Total		$389 40

Expenditures:
Mrs. Carrie B. Ware, postage	$2 93
Mr. Geo. King, Band	175 00
Ramblers' Orchestra, including 1 hr. extra	36 50
C. A. Brown, badges for sports	6 22

Anna Warner, tel. and stamps	1 85
Rudolph Stahl, feeding Band	33 00
D. L. Warner, ice cream, etc.	15 00
Transcript Printing Co.	19 75
Mrs. Clarke, singing	5 00

$295 25

Balance in treasury $94 15

Respectfully submitted,

BESSIE H. HANSON

Treasurer

ROAD AGENT'S REPORT

T. F. HUGRON IN ACCOUNT WITH THE TOWN OF HANCOCK

PAID FOR LABOR ON HIGHWAY 1928

March:

T. F. Hugron, labor, 76 hours	$42 18
T. F. Hugron, use of truck, 36½ hrs.	34 67
Chester Dufraine, labor, 29 hours	11 60
Laurence Dufraine, labor, 20 hours	8 00
M. I. Avery, labor, 8 hours	3 20
B. Dubois, labor, 1¼ hours	50
Harry Mulhall, team, 8 hours	6 22

$106 37

April:

T. F. Hugron, labor, 163 hours	$90 51
T. F. Hugron, use of truck, 168 hrs.	159 60
T. F. Hugron, for gas and oil	27 55
Chester Dufraine, labor, 153 hours	61 20
M. I. Avery, labor, 83 hours	33 20
David Coughlan, labor, 31 hours	12 40
Ephraim Wheeler, labor, 23 hours	9 20
Harry Dufraine, labor, 103 hours	41 20
Laurence Dufraine, labor, 119½ hours	47 80
Arthur Wheeler, labor, 11 hours	4 40
Fred Hugron, labor, 4 hours	1 60
C. Colby, labor, 4 hours	1 60
Harold Stearns, labor, 5 hours	2 00

Harold Stearns, with team, 56½ hours	43 94	
Joseph Hugron, with team, 4 hours	3 11	
Mulhall Bros., with team, 22½ hrs.	17 50	
Arthur Morton, with team, 4 hours	3 11	
Joe Quinn, with truck, 27 hours	36 00	
Arthur Wheeler, with truck, 71½ hours	95 33	
		$691 25

May:

T. F. Hugron, labor, 206 hours	$114 44	
T. F. Hugron, use of truck, 132 hrs.	125 40	
T. F. Hugron, for gas and oil	38 44	
Chester Dufraine, labor, 201 hours	80 40	
M. I. Avery, labor, 193 hours	77 20	
David Coughlan, labor, 63 hours	25 20	
Dan McDonald, labor, 51 hours	20 40	
Ephraim Wheeler, labor, 7 hours	2 80	
Sam Gilman, labor, 7 hours	2 80	
Melvin Loomis, labor, 11 hours	4 40	
Joe Quinn, with truck, 18 hours	24 00	
Arthur Wheeler, with truck, 59 hrs.	78 67	
Joseph Hugron, with truck, 10 hrs.	13 33	
Joseph Hugron, with team and extra man, 8 hours	10 60	
		$618 08

June:

T. F. Hugron, labor, 184 hours	$102 23	
T. F. Hugron, use of truck, 138 hrs.	119 16	
T. F. Hugron, gas and oil	13 76	
Chester Dufraine, labor, 183 hours	73 20	
M. I. Avery, labor, 179 hours	71 60	
Ernest Wood, labor, 147 hours	58 80	
M. S. Tuttle, labor, 9 hours	3 60	
Dan McDonald, labor, 16 hours	6 40	
Arthur Wheeler, with truck, 43 hrs.	48 22	
Laurence Mulhall, with team and extra man, 2½ hours	2 94	
Joe Quinn, with truck, 13 hours	17 33	
Joe Quinn, use of truck, 11 hours	10 77	
		$528 01

July:

T. F. Hugron, labor, 145 hours	$80 56
T. F. Hugron, use of truck, 58 hours	41 24
T. F. Hugron, gas and oil	36 52
Chester Dufraine, labor, 129 hours	51 60
M. I. Avery, labor, 171 hours	68 40
Ernest Wood, labor, 158 hours	63 20
Harold Stearns, with team, 20½ hours	15 96
Harold Stearns, labor, 2 hours	80

$358 28

August:

T. F. Hugron, labor, 155½ hours	$86 39
T. F. Hugron, use of truck, 151½ hours	107 73
T. F. Hugron, gas and oil	8 40
Chester Dufraine, labor, 133½ hrs.	53 40
M. I. Avery, labor, 164½ hours	65 80
Ernest Wood, labor, 88½ hours	35 40
M. Jones, labor, 9 hours	· 3 60
C. Colby, labor, 100½ hours	40 20
Arthur Wheeler with truck, 35 hrs.	38 89
Joe Quinn, with truck, 27 hours	30 00
Joe Hugron, with team, 18 hours	14 00
Harold Stearns, team and extra man	12 60

$496 41

September:

T. F. Hugron, labor, 137 hours	$76 11
T. F. Hugron, use of truck, 73 hrs.	51 91
T. F. Hugron, gas and oil .	16 68
Chester Dufraine, labor, 114 hours	45 60
M. I. Avery, labor, 132 hours	52 80
Ernest Wood, labor, 128 hours	51 20
C. Colby, labor, 132 hours	52 80
Arthur Wheeler, with truck, 18 hrs.	20 00

$367 10

October:

T. F. Hugron, labor, 42 hours	$23 33
T. F. Hugron, use of truck, 40 hrs.	28 44

M. I. Avery, labor, 36 hours	14 40	
Ernest Wood, labor, 40 hours	16 00	
C. Colby, labor, 23 hours	9 20	
Fred Hugron, labor, 27 hours	10 80	
Arthur Wheeler, with truck, 18 hrs.	20 00	
Joe Hugron, with truck, 18 hours	20 00	
Arthur Morton, team, 18 hours	14 00	
		$156 17

November:

T. F. Hugron, labor, 81 hours	$45 00	
T. F. Hugron, use of truck, 103½ hours	73 60	
T. F. Hugron, gas and oil	6 60	
Chester Dufraine, labor, 111½ hrs.	44 60	
M. I. Avery, labor, 72 hours	28 80	
Ernest Wood, labor, 115 hours	46 00	
C. Colby, labor, 60½ hours	24 20	
Sam Gilman, labor, 11½ hours	4 60	
Fred Wilder, with truck, 37 hours	41 12	
		$314 52

December:

T. F. Hugron, labor, 12 hours	$6 66	
T. F. Hugron, use of truck, 12 hours	8 53	
M. I. Avery, labor, 12 hours	4 80	
		$19 99

MATERIAL USED ON HIGHWAY

D. O. Devens, tools and supplies	$7 81
T. F. Hugron, repair on tractor	40 14
E. K. Upton, 6152 ft. bridge plank	184 56
Almon Hill, blacksmithing	2 24
North East Metal Culvert Co., 188 ft. 10x20, 12x20, 14x28 Metal pipe	213 92
John B. Varick Co., 20 ft. Metal pipe (10x30)	68 00
Geo. Wilder, dynamite, fuse and caps	4 40
C. A. Upton, nails	1 92
American Express Co., for express	2 22

T. F. Hugron, 73 posts	7	30
Ephraim Wheeler, 70 railings	17	50
Charles Adams, 381 loads gravel	38	10
Ernest Wood, 26 loads gravel	2	60
Fred Clark, 99 loads gravel	9	90
W. A. Osgood, 13 loads gravel	1	30
Clarence Ware, 53 loads gravel	5	30
James M. Cashion, 154 loads gravel	15	40
Carl Larson, 47 loads gravel	4	70
H. C. Wheeler, 206 loads gravel	20	60
Harry Sheldon, 240 loads gravel	24	00
John Reaveley, 229 loads gravel	22	90
Ephraim Weston, 4 loads gravel		40
Morris Fairfield, 34 loads gravel	3	40
Joe Hugron, 73 loads gravel	7	30
Mamie Jaquith, 24 loads gravel	2	40
Ephraim Wheeler, 32 loads gravel	3	20

$711 51

CLASS FIVE—MAIN HIGHWAYS AND BRIDGES

T. F. Hugron, Road Agent, in Account with Town of Hancock

Town maintenance, cash received from town treasurer	$4,367	69
R. B. Harrington	83	33
American Tar Co.	96	80

REPORT OF STORM DAMAGE AUGUST 19, 1928

T. F. Hugron, labor, 32 hours	$17	78
T. F. Hugron, use of truck, 5 hours	3	55
Chester Dufraine, labor, 19 hours	7	60
M. I. Avery, labor, 23 hours	9	20
Ernest Wood, labor, 33 hours	13	20
C. Colby, labor, 24 hours	9	60
Sam Gilman, labor, 5 hours	2	00
Charles Hoit, labor, 5 hours	2	00
F. Haas, labor, 3 hours	1	20
J. Haas, labor, 3 hours	1	20

Geo. Colby, labor, 5 hours	2 00	
Fred Bean, labor, 5 hours	2 00	
Fred Sheldon, labor, 5 hours	2 00	
Wm. Fisher, labor, 5 hours	2 00	
M. S. Tuttle, labor, 5 hours	2 00	
		$77 33

WINTER ROADS

DECEMBER AND JANUARY 1928 AND 1929

T. F. Hugron, labor, 46½ hours	$25 83	
T. F. Hugron, use of truck, 25½ hrs.	18 13	
M. I. Avery, labor, 28 hours	11 20	
Chester Dufraine, labor, 17 hours	6 80	
C. Colby, labor, 16 hours	6 40	
Ernest Wood, labor, 8 hours	3 20	
H. M. Sheldon, plowing sidewalks	8 20	
Mrs. Emma Vatcher, team breaking roads	60	
Fred Gleason for team	00	
Almon Hill, blacksmithing	8 25	
H. F. Nichols & Son, repairs on tractor	97 88	
		$197 49
R. B. Harrington		$40 08
F. E. Everett, balance State snow account.		$17 09

We have examined the accounts of the Treasurer of the Common Fund, Water Commissioners, Electric Light Committee, Town Treasurer, Trustees of Trust Funds, Selectmen, Tax Collector, Road Agent, Overseer of the Poor and Town Clerk and find them correctly cast and properly vouched. We have examined the accounts of the Library Trustees and find an error of $0.25 in the balance. We find a balance in the hands of the Town Treasurer of $3,900.09; balance in the hands of the Treasurer of the Common Fund of $1.70; and balance in the hands of the Treasurer of the Library of $175.12.

GEORGE W. GOODHUE
KARL G. UPTON
Auditors

REPORT OF THE SUPERINTENDENT OF SCHOOLS

TO THE HANCOCK SCHOOL BOARD

On the basis of expenditure per thousand dollars of equalized valuation, Hancock has dropped from the 188th out of 252 school districts in New Hampshire, to the 120th out of 244 school districts. This has been done without pupils suffering for educational facilities. But the point remains that during those years, more than sixty New Hampshire towns have passed by Hancock in the total costs per wealth, or their schools.

This can be more simply stated by the comment that some sixty towns are investing more on school child welfare, in comparison with their wealth, than was the case when Hancock was expending $9.15 out of each thousand dollars of her equalized valuation.

Rigid economy must always be balanced against strictly thrifty habits, and the decision must be in favor of the latter. The School Board of Hancock shows no attitude against wise expenditure; but has succeeded in changing from certain expensive-in-the-long-run plans to such as will, over a period of years, give a lower per pupil cost.

Of particular interest this year is the purchasing of supplies for the towns of Supervisory Union No. 47 on a basis of total needs. This has brought to the small towns, for the first time, economies both of purchase and delivery. Purchases in volume sufficient to care for the standard needs of six towns lowered the item by item cost in many instances by as much as fifty per cent., when month by month or small amount purchasing was the rule.

No town is required to share in the buying, but any town that so desires may take advantage of the lowered costs.

Central office methods, supplying school needs for particular standardized ratings, have cut the cost in what is, next to the teaching, the most important part of the school's function, the assurance to parents and tax payers that children in Hancock shall have equal or better opportunity than those in city school systems.

None of these matters which make it possible for Hancock, and the other small towns in this Supervisory Union, to maintain superior schools, could be carried to their present efficiency were it not for the fact that the teaching staff and all officially connected individuals are apparently working together in complete harmony.

Three schools were maintained for a full year. The budget has been balanced for both revenue and outlay.

(Signed)   LAWTON CHASE

REPORT OF THE SCHOOL BOARD TO THE CITIZENS

OF HANCOCK

FINANCIAL REPORT JULY 1, 1927 TO JUNE 30, 1928

Cora F. Otis, salary	$30 00	
Check list and supervision	3 00	
		$33 00
Wm. D. Fogg, salary	$25 00	
Check list and supervision	3 00	
		$28 00
Ella C. Ware, salary	$30 00	
Check list and supervision	3 00	
		$33 00
Nellie M. Welsh, clerk		$5 00
E. L. Adams, treasurer	$20 00	
Postage and stationery	2 10	
		$22 10
Superintendent's excess salary	$236 11	
State tax	170 00	
		$406 11
Auditors:		
Karl Upton	$2 00	
G. W. Goodhue	2 00	
		$4 00
Teachers' salaries:		
Nellie M. Welsh	$788 89	
Anna T. Wallace	850 00	
Evelyn Harrison	1,150 00	
Beth Adams, music	36 00	
Mamie Harrington	34 00	
Elizabeth Welch	17 00	
Ellen Weston	183 31	
		$3,059 20

Expenses of administration	$51 18	
Text books	113 63	
Scholars' supplies	100 86	
Expenses of instructions	21 30	
Janitor	275 00	
Fuel	249 79	
Janitor supplies	44 03	
Repairs	76 97	
Medical inspection	50 00	
Transportation	1,943 20	
Special activities	26 00	
Flag	5 00	
High School tuition	2,350 00	
Smith Hughes	593 18	
		$5,900 14
Notes and interest on debt		$1,100 93
		$10,591 48

SCHOOL BOARD'S BUDGET FOR 1929-30

SCHOOL DISTRICT OF HANCOCK

Support of Schools:

Teachers' salaries	$3,200 00	
Text books	115 00	
Scholars' supplies	125 00	
Flags and appurtenances	5 00	
Other expenses of instruction	30 00	
Janitor service	275 00	
Fuel	250 00	
Water, light, janitors' supplies	45 00	
Minor repairs and expenses	75 00	
Health supervision (Med. Insp.)	50 00	
Transportation of pupils	2,000 00	
Other special activities	30 00	
		$6,200 00

Other Statutory Requirements:

Salaries of District Officers (Fixed by District)	$150 00	
Truant Officer and School Census (Fixed by District)	8 00	

TREASURER'S ACCOUNT, SCHOOL DISTRICT
HANCOCK

Ernest L. Adams, Treasurer, in Account with the School
District of Hancock for the year, June 30, 1927-June 30, 1928
Received:
1927

July 1, Balance on hand	$22 40
July 15, State Treasurer Smith Hughes	593 18
Sept. 30, E. L. Adams, treasurer, School money	1,200 00
Oct. 26, E. L. Adams, treasurer, School money	1,000 00
Nov. 21, E. L. Adams, treasurer, School money	1,800 00
Dec. 19, E. L. Adams, treasurer, School money	500 00
Dec. 19, C. R. Welsh, school house	10 00
1928	
Jan. 3, E. L. Adams, treasurer, School money	1,200 00
Jan. 3, Evelina C. A. Reavely, school house	15 00
Jan. 3, W. D. Fogg, stoves sold	7 00
Jan. 15, State Treasurer, education equalization	733 58
Jan. 25, W. E. Putnam, school house	10 00
Feb. 1, W.D. Fogg, paint, oil sold	20 00
Feb. 1, E. L. Adams, treasurer, School money	3,059 66
Feb. 25, Ephraim Weston, school house	10 00
June 19, E. L. Adams, treasurer, license money	83 73
June 19, E. L. Adams, treasurer, School money	350 00
June 27, Ella Ware, for windows	2 00

Total receipts	$10,616 55
Total School Board orders	10,591 48
Balance on hand	$25 07

ERNEST L. ADAMS, Treasurer

Payment of tuitions in High Schools and Academies (Estimated by Board)	2,800 00	
Superintendent's Excess Salary (Fixed by Supervisory Union)	250 00	
Per Capita Tax (Reported by State Treasurer)	198 00	
Other Obligations	75 00	
		$3,481 00
Total amount required to meet School Board's Budget		$9,681 00

ESTIMATED INCOME OF DISTRICT

State Aid (Dec. 1928 allotment)	$500 00	
Dog Tax (Estimate)	175 00	
Elementary School tuition receipts (Estimate)	36 00	
Deduct total estimated income (not raised by taxation)		$711 00
Assessment required to balance School Board's Budget		$8,970 00

CORA F. OTIS
WILLIAM D. FOGG
ELLA C. WARE
School Board

February 4, 1929
Hancock, N. H.

To apply for state aid $5,895.76 must be raised for elementary schools.

REPORT OF TREASURER OF TRUSTEES

F. PEARSON

Received during fiscal year:
On hand Feb. 1, 1928:

On deposit in Peterborough Nat'l Bank	$184 84	
Cash in hand	1 59	

Fines during fiscal year	14 39	
Interest on Helen J. Davis bonds	100 00	
Income from trust funds as per report of trustees of trust funds	474 28	
From reserve fund	200 00	
From sale of town history and cemetery books	14 80	
Total receipts		$989 90
Paid out during fiscal year:		
Librarian's salary	$187 68	
Janitor's salary	125 00	
Lighting	27 20	
Fuel—coal, wood and kindling	221 72	
Periodicals for reading room	56 00	
Books and reports	80 56	
Bonding magazines and books	54 70	
Paid town treasurer, sales of town and cemetery books	14 80	
Fire hose and labor	22 61	
Waxing floors	11 75	
Incidental supplies	13 01	
Balance in Peterborough Nat'l Bank Feb. 1, 1929	174 87	
Total expenditures		$989 90
Reserve fund, Peterborough Savings Bank		$1,749 99
Heber J. Davis bonds		$2,000 00

Itemized accounts are in treasurer's book, audited by town auditors.

REPORT OF LIBRARY TRUSTEES

The trustees of the Hancock Town Library submit the following report:

Library and reading room open Tuesday, Thursday and Saturday from 2 to 5 and 6 to 9 P. M., legal holidays excepted.

There have been 342 charge cards issued, representing 4339 adult and 1300 juvenile volumes, and 1173 periodicals taken out.

Mrs. Minnie S. Ware, who served so efficiently as member and treasurer of the trustees since 1910, passed from this life July 4th. Later Miss Margaret Perry was appointed to serve out her unexpired term.

The trustees had Mr. W. D. Fogg install a fire hose for emergency protection.

Owing to the increased cost of books, periodicals, and especially the increased cost of heating the enlarged library, the trustees find the income from the invested funds insufficient and have been obliged to use $200 from the reserve fund. It is unwise to do this for current expenses, so the trustees respectfully submit that if the library is to serve the community as efficiently as it should, the town should make a yearly appropriation of at least $200.

The Library has been very fortunate this year in the matter of gifts. We have received several valuable and interesting books, amongst others, the Encyclopaedia Brittanica, Poems, etc.

The following is the list of those who have kindly remembered us with gifts, books and periodicals:

Mr. Everett Adams, Mr. and Mrs. George E. Bates, Dr. L. Vernon Briggs, Mrs. Maro S. Brooks, Miss F. Helen Carr, Mrs. Dorothy Clark, Mrs. Daniel Devens, Mrs. and Miss Dickerman, Mr. George Doyle, Mrs. Lucy C. Eaton, Mrs. Helen F. Fowle, Mr. Frank F. Fowle, Mrs. Esther Gardner, Miss Gertrude Gleason, Mr. and Mrs. George W. Goodhue, Mr. and Mrs. Chester Green, Mrs. Sarah C. Haydon, Mr. Arthur C. Hayes, Mrs. Hannah Kimball, Mrs. Joseph D. Leland, Mrs. T. Bertram Manning, Mr. and Mrs. Arthur Morton, Rev. Frank Pearson, Miss Margaret Perry, Col. Arthur J. Pierce, Mrs. Bertus Pietersz, Mr. Henry N. Rice, Mrs. Gardner Rockwood, Miss Christine Rockwood, Mrs. Ruth T. Sheedy, Mr. Stuart R. Sheedy, Mr. Waldermere Stahl, Mr. and Mrs. Foster Stearns, Miss Mary Tenney,

Mr. and Mrs. Edson K. Upton, Mrs. Ida Weeden, Mr. George M. Wilder, Mrs. Carrie A. Wilds, Mrs. Alvah M. Wood, Mr. Ernest Wood.

Number of volumes reported Feb. 1, 1928	8992
Number of volumes added by trustees	52
Number of volumes acquired by gift	169
Whole number Feb. 1, 1929	9213

List of Books Added to Library 1928

REPORTS

Librarian of Congress	026.5.1
N. H. Bank	353.1
N. H. Bureau of Labor	353.1
N. H. Highway	353.1
N. H. Insurance	353.1
N. H. Law Enforcement	353.1
N. H. Manual for the general court	310.2
N. H. Public Service Commission	353.1
N. H. State Board of Charities	353.1
N. H. State School	353.1
N. H. State Tax Commission	353.1
The Encyclopaedia Britannica, 29 vols.	030.4

ETHICS

Briggs	
Occupation versus restraint	131.2
Schauffler	
Peter Pantheism	147.1

THEOLOGY

Bates	
Seen and unseen	212.3
Besant	
Man's life in this and other worlds	212.4
Man's life in three worlds ·	212.10
Burgess	
Baptism	265.1B
Fallows	
The home beyond	237.5
Keller	
My religion	204.26
Krishnamurti .	
The pool of wisdom	212.13
Larsen .	
My travels in the spirit world	212.11
Leadbeater	
The other side of death	212.12
Owen	
The battalions of heaven	212.9
The highlands of heaven	212.7
The lowlands of heaven	212.6
The ministry of heaven	212.8
Sinnett	
In the next world	212.5
Smith	
Some timeless messages of the Christian faith	230.15

SOCIOLOGY

Baldwin	
Fairy stories and fables	398.4.1A
Briggs	
History of the Psychopathic Hospital, Boston, Mass.	362.2.1
Conwell	
Acres of diamonds	331.85.2
Cook	
American Institutions	321.07.4.3
Grimm	
Fairy tales	398.4.4A

Medical Department of the U. S. Army in World
    War, 3 vols.   353.6.2
Murasaki
    The tale of the Genii   398.4.7
Rukeyser
    Money and investment   332.5

PHILOLOGY

Griel
    Glimpses of Nature for little folks   428.2.4
Tomkins
    Universal Indian sign language   497.1

SCIENCE

Denton
    Real out-of-door stories   590.33
Miller
    Old red sandstone   550.12
Williams
    The evolution of man scientifically disproved   575.10

USEFUL ARTS

Chase
    Your money's worth   614.3.1
Holt
    Encyclopaedia of household economy   640.2

FINE ARTS

Arthur
    Embroidery book   746.26
King
    The little garden   710.3

LITERATURE

Bacheller	
Best things in American literature	810.8
Davis	
The old stone hitching post	811.4.57
Longfellow	
Poetical works, 2 vols.	811.34.12
Masterpieces of American eloquence	808.18
Moore	
The challenge of life	810.9
Stearns	
The transplanting	826.8
Underwood	
English literature	820.14

BIOGRAPHY

Byrd	
Skyward	BB26.1
Horn	
Trader Horn	BH19.1
Irwin	
Herbert Hoover	BH20.1
Maurois	
Disraeli	BD12.1
Ticknor	
May Alcott	BA3.2

COLLECTIVE BIOGRAPHY

Fraser	
Reminiscences of a Diplomatist's wife	920.04.2
Howe	
Memories of a hostess	920.68
Willets	
Rulers of the world at home	923.14

History and Travel

Boylston	
Sister	940.9.32
Briggs	
Around Cape Horn to Honolulu	919.6.4
Carpenter	
Alaska, our northern wonderland	917.98.3
From Tangier to Tripoli	916.16
Claridge	
Wild bush tribes of tropical Africa	916.15
Dunbar	
History of travel in America, 4 vols.	917.10
Eldredge	
Beginnings of San Francisco, 2 vols.	979.4.6
Griggs	
The valley of ten thousand smokes	917.9
Hills	
The golden river	918.10
Hubbard	
A woman's way through unknown Labrador	971.9.5
Meech	
This generation	942.19
Pillsbury	
New Hampshire History, 5 vols.	974.2.15
Powell	
The new frontiers of freedom	914.18
Sharp	
The better country	917.94.1
Sheridan	
West and East	914.17
Slaughter	
Heirs of old Venice	945.5
Wallace	
The lure of the Labrador wild	971.9.4

Fiction

Bacheller	
In the days of Poor Richard	B2.12A
Bailey	
The dim lantern	B74.2A

Rinehart	
Two flights up	R33.14
Sage	
The jolly ten	S104.1
Smith	
A gentleman vagabond	S6.2A
Smith	
Pollyanna's debt of honor	S82.4
Pollyanna's Jewels	S82.3
Somerville	
French leave	S102.1
Spyri	
Jorli.	S30.6
Standish	
Lefty Locke	S101.1
The man on first	S101.2
Stephens	
Etched in moonlight	S103.1
Tarkington	
Beasley's Christmas party	T6.14
Thompson	
The battle of the horizons	T49.1
Van Vechten	
Spider Boy	V14.1
Weale	
China's crucifixion	W88.1
Webster	
Mary Wollaston	W57.2
Wells	
Prillilgirl	W31.27
Wilder	
The bridge of San Luis Rey.	W87.1
Willsie.	
The enchanted canyon	W74.1A
Wright	
A son of his father	W61.12
Books rebound, 12 volumes	

Magazines rebound:

Century, 4 vols.

Granite Monthly, 2 vols.

Harper's, 4 vols.

National Geographic, 4 vols.

Scribner's, 4 vols.

St. Nicholas, 4 vols.

World's Work, 4 vols.

PERIODICALS

American
American Issue
Century
Child Life
Christian Herald
Congregationalist
Country Life
Delineator
Elks
Farm and Fireside
Farmer's wife
Fruits and Garden
Good Housekeeping
Granite Monthly
Harper's
Hunter, Trader, Trapper
Hygeia
Junior Home
Ladies' Home Journal
Life
Literary Digest
National Geographic
National Republic
Needlecraft
Outlook
People's Home Journal
Peterborough Transcript
Pictorial Review
Popular Mechanics
Review of Reviews
Rural New Yorker
Scientific American
Scribner's
St. Nicholas
Woman's Home Companion
World's Work
Youth's Companion

LIBRARY BUILDING COMMITTEE REPORT

The Committee regret that, owing to circumstances which made it impossible to get the help necessary for work on the roof, their final report cannot be submitted at this time.

We were able, however, to complete the re-location of curbing on the lawn and necessary grading preparatory to setting of the balance of the shrubs.

Respectfully submitted,
CHARLES E. ADAMS
MARGARET PERRY
WILLIAM E. PUTNAM
Library Building Committee

Report of Trust Funds of the Town of Hancock, N. H., on February 1, 1929

Date of Creation	Trust Funds — Name of Creation	How Invested	Amount of Principal	Rate of Interest	Balance of Income on Hand at Beginning of Year	Income During Year	Paid during Year	Balance of Income on Hand at End of Year
1889	Abb Legacy—Support of Library—Aol hs Whitcomb	Hancock Town Ns	$4000 00	3½				
		Mr Savings Bank	1000 00	4½				
		ng Savings Bank	2000 00	4½				
		New ore Savings Bank	2000 00	4½				
1889	Wb Legacy—Care of Common— As Mb	ore Savings Bank	00 00	4		$383 46	$383 46	$5 @ 19
		Hancock Gn Ns	4300 00	4				
1872	Hubbard Legacy—Support of Library— Dr Hd	Mr Savings Bank	700 00	4½	$438 61	215 58	150 00	
		Mr Savings Bank	200 00	4½				
1872	Hubbard Legacy—Benefit Town Poor— Ebenezer Hubbard	Hancock Gn N de	800 0	4		41 03	41 03	
		Hancock Gn N de	500 00	4	201 68	51 90	95 00	158 58
1879	My Legacy—Support of Library—Abijah	Peterboro Sgs Bank	500 00	4½				
1883	Salina Hills Memorial Fund—Support of ny	do Savings Bank	1000 00	4½		45 50	45 50	
1896	Asa Gordon By Shol Library—Salina Hills	Peterboro Savings Bank	200 00	4½		9 10	9 10	
	By School Fund—Support of S. By School Library—Asa Gn	Peterboro Savings Bk	100 00	4½		4 54	4 54	
1906	Nct Mt Un fry Fund—Harriet Harriet M. fn	Peterboro Sgs Bank	100 00	4½	28 16	5 82	6 75	27 23
1908	Gn Nn fetery Fund—Oren Nelson	Peterboro Savings aBk	50 00	4½	3 77	2 42	2 75	3 44
1909	Hn An Cemetery Fund—Johan	Peterboro Savings Bank	100 00	4½	38 97	6 29	8 75	36 51
1910	Zopher W. Bs fry Fund—Zopher W. Brooks	do Gs Bank	50 00	4½	9 17	2 67	3 25	8 59
1913	C. W. & H E. Hirn efery Fund— Hes W. & Mry E. Mrn	Peterboro Savings Bank	100 00	4½	4 01	4 72	2 50	6 23
1913	Sarah A. Fairbanks fry Fund—Sarah A. bks	hiboro Savings ak	00 00	1½	30 44	5 91	10 00	26 35
1913	Un fry Fund—Julia A. Joslin	hiboro as aBk	50 00	4½	17 32	7 59	8 00	16 91
1914	Rosamond Brooks Fund—Purchase of books	Peterboro Savings Bk	00 00	4½	147 01	24 87	15 25	156 63
1916	for Gn Library—Sevi Brooks Rev. W. W. Hayward fry Fund—Ellen	do Sgs Bank	100 00	4½	4 54	4 54	4 54	
1918	Ha Wood fetery Fund—Joshua Wood Hayward	Peterboro Sgs Bk	30 00	4½	14 82	2 00	5 50	11 32
1918	Albert Shedd fetery Fund—Albert Shedd	Peterboro as Bk	40 00	4½	4 94	2 02	1 75	5 21
		do as Bank	100 00	4½	14 51	5 19	5 00	14 70

Year	Name / Fund	Bank	Principal	Rate				
1919	...h A. Tarbell ...y Fund—J...ph	Peterboro Savings Bank	100 00	4½	19 68		5 41	6 50	18 59
1 99	A. ...ll ...n ...n ...y	Peterboro Savings Bank	1000 00	4½	209 77		55 00	26 00	38 77
1 99	C. M. ...n ...n ...y Fund—C. M. Shel-	...o Savings Bank	200 00	4½	53 83		11 52	5 75	59 60
1920	Cyrus R. ...dn ...ls ...y Fund—Flora	...o Savings Bank	50 00	4½	10 02		2 72	2 00	10 74
1922	M. Dunn L. ...n ...ll ...y Fund—L. ...tn	Peterboro Savings Bank	100 00	4½	13 86		5 14	5 25	13 75
1922	L. Kimball ...en ...ll ...ny ...Bg	First N...nal Bank, Peterboro			1 55				1 55
1923	Library—L. ...n Andrew C. Cochrane W. N ...ne	...o ...ags Bank	10 00	4½	2 0...		54		2 55
1923	P. B. ...ne Wn & A. ...Hill ...y Fund—	...o Savings Bank	00 00	4½	10 88		5 01	4 50	11 39
1923	Ms. P. B. ...Wn ...y Fund—Martha ...d Emerson Ae ...Hn	...o Savings Bank	50 00	4½	6 81		2 56	1 00	8 37
1923	...ad ...r Foster ...y Fund—Elwin C.	...Nr Savings Bank	50 00	4½	3 86		2 45		6 31
1923	...r J. Davis Davis ...y Fund—Heber J.	...Nr Savings ...Bk	00 00	4½	24 97		10 17	8 75	26 39
1924	...e H. Ware ...y ...e	...o Savings Bank	00 00	4½	12 90		5 10	2 00	16 00
1925	H. Ware ...At M. Dodge ...y Fund—A...dt	Peterboro Savings Bank	50 00	4½	4 96		2 47		7 43
1925	M. Dodge ...Bd ...y ...ll	...bo Savings Bank	30 00	4½	3 68		1 50	50	4 68
1926	...Viola M. ...der ...dr ...y Fund—Viola M	...bo Savings Bank	100 00	4½	6 63		4 83		11 46
1926	W. H. ...h ...n ...Be ...y Fund—W. H. Wes-	Peterboro Savings Bank	100 00	4½	5 91		4 78	1 00	9 69
1927	...h J. ...Bd J. Bullard ...y Fund—Hannah	Peterboro Savings Bank	50 00	4½	1 00		2 31		3 31
1927	...Hn S. ...fn ...y Fund—Helen	...lg Savings Bank	100 00	4½			3 00		3 00
1928	Ha... ...he Lee ...y Fund—Elsie	Peterl ...o Savings Bank	50 00	4½			1 84		1 84
1928	D. Lee Cyrus H. ...Bk ...y Fund—Cyrus		100 00						
1928	H. Philbrick ...n Hill ...y Fund—Almon Hill	Peterboro Savings Bank	125 00	4½			2 50		2 50
1928	...n of ...Bk Electric ...Bg ...Bg	Peterboro Savings Bank	200 00	4½			6 54		6 54
	Fund	...o ...gs Bank					800 00		60 00

TOWN WARRANT

THE STATE OF NEW HAMPSHIRE

To the Inhabitants of the Town of Hancock in the County
of Hillsborough, in said State, qualified to vote in
Town Affairs:

You are hereby notified to meet at Town Hall in said
Hancock on Tuesday, the Twelfth day of March next, at
nine of the clock in the forenoon, to act upon the following
subjects:

1. To choose all necessary Town officers for the ensuing
year.

2. To raise such sums of money as may be necessary to
defray town charges for the ensuing year, and make appro-
priation for the same.

3. To see if the town will vote to accept the provisions
of Chapter 87, Section 1 of the Public Statutes on a Section
of the Contoocook Valley road so called, and appropriate
or set aside from the amount raised for the highway work
the sum of

4. To see how much money the town will vote to raise or
appropriate for the proper observance of Memorial Day.

5. To see how much money the town will vote to raise
or appropriate for the proper observance of Old Home Day
and the celebration of the town Sesqui-Centennial.

6. To see if the town will vote to buy a Blake snow plow
with attachments to mount on a motor truck and raise and
appropriate money for the same.

7. To see if the town will vote to buy for the Fire Department 300 feet 3 inch hose or pass any vote relating thereto.

8. To see if the town will grant the Congregational
Church the right to place a motor near the northwest corner
of the Town Hall and run an iron pipe therefrom through the
ceiling to their room above when they install a new pipe organ
in their church.

9. To see if the town will vote to instruct or authorize
the Electric Lighting Committee to make a new contract
with the Public Service Co. of New Hampshire, or take any
action relating thereto.

10. To see if the town will vote to extend the electric lighting system, take any action relating thereto and raise and appropriate money for the same.

11. To see if the town will vote to authorize and instruct the Electric Lighting Committee to include any additions that may be made to the electric line during 1929 in the sale of its electric light lines as already authorized or take any action relating thereto.

12. To see if the town will vote to extend the water line from hydrant just north of Ernest L. Adams' residence to residence of Laurence Dufrain and raise and appropriate money for the same or take any action relating thereto.

13. To see if the town will vote to put in water from Ernest L. Adams corner to M. A. Foote house and raise and appropriate money for the same.

14. To see if the town will vote to raise and appropriate the sum of one hundred fifty dollars to be used for the erection of suitable new guide boards and repainting old ones where possible including the two Publicity signs.

15. To see if the town will vote to raise and appropriate the sum of Five Hundred Dollars, said sum to be expended for permanent improvement of the so-called middle road to Peterborough and to be laid out on said road from the village to the Peterborough line by way of Mrs. Lindsley's and the Hayward Farms and said sum is understood to be over and above the amount of money that may be allotted to this section of road for usual repairs and upkeep.

16. To see if the town will vote to raise and appropriate the sum of Four Hundred Dollars for suppression of the White Pine Blister Rust.

17. To hear the reports of agents, auditors and committees and pass any vote relating thereto.

18. To transact any other business that may legally come before said meeting.

Given under our hands and seal, this twenty-third day of February, in the year of our Lord nineteen hundred and twenty-nine.

GEORGE H. FOGG
MAURICE S. TUTTLE
CHARLES E. ADAMS
Selectmen of Hancock

Date 1928	Name of Child	Sex	Living or sb	No. of child	Name of Father	Maiden Name of Mother	Residence of Parents	Occupation of Father	Birthplace of Father	Birthplace of Mother
June 5	■el ■ ra Loomis	F	L	1	Melvin Loomis	Florence Hill	Hancock, N.H.	Truckman	Hancock, N. H.	Greenfield, N. H.
Aug. 8	William ■n, Jr.	M	L	1	William ■on	Esther B. Wright	Hancock, N.H.	Farmer	Hancock, N. H.	Unity, N. H.
Sept. 10	■la Rose ■te	F	L	6	William L. ■te	Rose A. LeMarie	Hancock, N.H.	R.R. Section	Nova Scotia	Magog, Canada
Oct. 20	Grant D. Bumford	M	L	10	■e Bumford	Beth Duell	Hancock, N.H.	Laborer	Hillsboro, N. H.	Warn e, N. H.
Oct. 20	Gloria M. Bumford	F	L	11	George Bumford	Beth Duell	Hancock, N.H.	Laborer	Hillsboro, N. H.	Warn e, N. H.
Nov. 13	Marguerite L. Johnson	F	L	5	Lester M. Johnson	Marguerite Hart	Hancock, N.H.	Carpenter	Hancock, N. H.	Manchester, N. H.
Nov. 24	Elsie Marie McInnis	F	L	2	Daniel McInnis	Elsie Holmes	Hancock, N.H.	Laborer	Nova Scotia	Berlin, Mo.

Marriages Registered in the Town of Hancock, N. H., for the Year Ending December 31, 1928

Place & Date of Marriage	Name and Surname of Groom and Bride	Residence of each at time of Marriage	Age	Occupation	Place of Birth of Each	Names of Parents	Place of Parents	Name, Residence and Official Station of Person by whom Married
1928 Jan. 13	William Weston	Hancock, N. H.	29	Farmer	Hancock, N. H.	Ephraim Weston / Agnes DeLong	Hancock, N. H. / Boston, Mass.	William Weston, Clergyman
Unity	Esther B. Wright	Unity, N. H.	21	Domestic	Unity, N. H.	Homer F. Wright / Annie L. Rowe	Unity, N. H. / Sun, N. H.	Unity, Md, N. H.
Feb. 4	Grant Twyne	Hancock, N. H.	21	Sawyer	Granville, N. Y.	F. A. Twyne / Ida Corey	Danby, Vt. / Pawlet, Vt.	C. Raymond Chappel Minister of Gospel Keene, N. H.
Keene	Ruth L. Farwell	Hancock, N. H.	20	Factory worker	Lincoln, N. H.	Frank C. Farwell / Lilian Hill	East Harrisville, N. H. / Dover, N. H.	
May 5	Leslie H. Wright	Hancock, N. H.	31	Laborer	Unity, N. H.	Homer F. Wright / Annie L. Rowe	Unity, N. H. / Sun, N. H.	William West a Clergyman Md, N. H.
Third	Mary E. Weston	Hancock, N. H.	24	At home	Boston, Mass.	Ephraim Weston / Agnes DeLong	Hancock, N. H. / Boston, Mass.	
June 21	Haydn S. Pearson	Hancock, N. H.	27	Teacher	Farmington, N. H	Frank P. Pearson / Rose R. Sanborn	Newburyport, Mass. / Holderness, N. H.	Frank Pearson, Clergyman Hancock, N. H.
Hancock	Ella M. Elliott	Ayer, Mass.	27	Secretary	Sawyerville, Que	Emil J. Elliott / Esther A. Lowry	Westbury, Que. / Low Forest, Que.	
June 30	Charlesworth Neilson	Ayer, Mass.	25		Hartford, Ct.	Frederick C. Neilson / Florence C. Keeney	Hartford, Ct. / Rhea, Pa.	Ernest W. Eldridge, Clergyman Hancock, N. H.
Hancock	Cynthia Shaw		23	Teacher	New York City	Joseph T. Shaw / Harriett Richardson	Gorham, Me. / Manchester, N. H.	
Aug. 22	Charles S. Bradley	Sun, N. H.	22	Accountant	Manchester, N. H.	Frederick W. Bradley / Jessie L. Babcock	Manchester, N. H. / Wilmot, N. H.	Carl D. Skilling, Clergyman Sun, S. R. I.
Hancock	Bessie L. Fogg	Hancock, N. H.	21	At home	Hancock, N. H.	William D. Fogg / Annie A. Hayward	Hancock, N. H. / Hancock, N. H.	
Aug. 29	Adam G. Shier	Hancock, N. H.	34	Farming	Phillipston, Mass.	Jason L. Fisher / Mary E. Goddard	Royalston, Mass / Richmond, N. H.	Earl F. Nauss, region Phila, N. H.
Nashua	Lena S. Finan	Hancock, N. H.	39	Housekeeper	Hancock, N. H.	Alfred A. Sellon	Hancock, N. H.	
Aug. 30	Chester F. Dutton	Hancock, N. H.	27	Auctioneer	Greenfield, N. H.	Orissa J. Lee / Ezra R. Dutton	Greenfield, N. H. / Sun, N. H.	Frank Pearson, Clergyman Hancock, N. H.
Hancock	Mabel W. Pearson	Hancock, N. H.	26	Teacher	Farmington, N. H	Nellie R. Fogg / Frank Pearson / Rose R. Sanborn	Harrisville, N. H. / Newburyport, Mass. / Holderness, N. H.	
Nov. 10	William P. Marr	Hyde Park, Mass.	22	Tel. Operator	Jamaica Plain, Mass.	Arthur N. Marr / Rhoda I. Polson	Lawrence, Mass. / Gardiner, Me.	Ernest W. Eldridge, Clergyman Hancock, N. H
Hancock	Annabelle Peacock	Hyde Park, Mass.	22	Salesman		Benjamin A. Peacock / Janie J. Hinan	Ireland	
Dec. 23	Daniel L. McDonald	Manchester	34	Shoeworker	N. H.	Leroy D. McDonald / Katherine McKensie	Manchester, N. H. / Portland, Me.	Ernest A. Marr, Minister Manchester, N. H.
Manchester	Ruth Wheeler	Hancock, N. H.	19	At home	Brookline, N. H.	Ephraim Wheeler / Bessie Smith	Mass, N. Y. / Md, N. H.	

Deaths Registered in the Town of Hancock, N. H., for the Year Ending December 31, 1928

Date 1928	Name	Years	Months	Days	Place of Birth	Sex M or W	S or Wid	Occupation	Place of Birth — Father	Place of Birth — Mother	Name of Father	Men Name of Mr
Mar. 1	rutie S. Ash	42	11	26	Hnak	F	S	At hme	atd	Ireland	Hfias E. Welsh	Ellen Kith
Mr. 13	Ma Kennard	83	2	26	Porter, Me.	F	W	Housekeeper			Jas Brl	Hannah Garland
June 12	Ephraim A. Muler	49	2	27	Moores Forks	M	M	Farmer		Weston, Vt.	Gs J. Wheeler	Lucy Aird
Aug. 14	Nellie J. Tuttle	78	8	6	Hancock	F	W	At home	feeGd	Newbury, N. H.	Eli M.	Betsey Jnett
Aug. 15	Emily A. Sheldon	83	11	17	Antrim, N. H.	F	W	At home	atN. H.	England	M. opon	Melita Kigm
Nov. 4	Evelina Reaveley	84		20	England	F	W		England	Wtr, N. H.	Davis	Mth Mll
Nov. 9	Donald G. Bumford				Hancock, N. H.	M			Hi'lsboro, N. H.		George Bumford	

Brought to Town for Burial

Date 1928	Name	Years	Months	Days	Place of Birth	Sex M or W	S or Wid	Occupation	Place of Birth — Father	Place of Birth — Mother	Name of Father	Men Name of Mr
Jan. 13	Myron E. Jeon	70	2	17	Hancock, N. H.	M	M	Niht	Hancock, N. H	1 Mo, N. H.	James W. 1 Jan	Mry A. Sawyer
eb. 15	Alex. Elin	50	5	18	Wake'd, Ms.	M	S	atler	Wwn	dwn	D. R. Mon	Ellen Mry
Mar. 4	Anie M. ogils	84	6	9	Hancock, N. H.	F					Hgah Mirn	Betsey F May
Mar. 11	George E. Blake	78	3	14	Alexandria	M	S	Retired farmer	Newport, R. I.	Hancock, N. H.	I. Ms Blake	Frances Sargent
May 7	Thomas S. Perry	83	8	8	Newport, R. I.	M	M	Per	figh, Ms.	Philadelphia, Pa.	Christopher G. Perry	Phedora W. Priest
June 18	Mry E. Hill	80	5	29	Wn, N. H.	F	W	eier	San, N. H.	Hancock, N. H.	Jason Blanchard	Ida A. Man
July 18	Ge W. Ware	30	4	24	Bennington	M	M	At	Hancock, N. H.	Dummerston, Vt.	Ed Won	Sarah Laughton
July 4	Me S. Ware	68	1	22	Hnak, N. H.	F	S	Md	Hancock, N. H.	orth, N. H.	Gardner Knight	Man Gin
Ag. 12	Ieten M. Higns	88	1	11	Hnak, N. H.	H		atk	Hnak, N. H.	Weare, N. H	Willis oSte Mon	Etta Lull Mnh
Nov. 20	Ge E. Johnson	24	3	18	Deering, N. H.	F	W	rbe	Deering, N. H.	Milford, N. H.	J nas Ellin wod	Rachel G. rfir

CPSIA information can be obtained
at www.ICGtesting.com
Printed in the USA
BVHW061226081118
532530BV00007B/208/P